# Muslim
## Mosque

*For Rizwaan and Maleeha Malik*

**For a free color catalog describing Gareth Stevens' list of high-quality books and multimedia programs, call 1-800-542-2595 (USA) or 1-800-461-9120 (Canada). Gareth Stevens Publishing's Fax: (414) 225-0377.**

Gareth Stevens Publishing thanks Reverend Robert W. Lambeck, S. J., for his assistance with the accuracy of the text. Father Lambeck, a Jesuit priest, is Assistant Professor of Theology at Marquette University, Milwaukee, Wisconsin. He was a regular participant in a Muslim-Christian dialogue group that met on a monthly basis for more than ten years.

Library of Congress Cataloging-in-Publication Data available upon request from publisher.
Fax: (414) 225-0377 for the attention of the Publishing Records Department.

ISBN 0-8368-2609-4

This North American edition first published in 2000 by
**Gareth Stevens Publishing**
1555 North RiverCenter Drive, Suite 201
Milwaukee, WI 53212 USA

Original edition © 1998 by Franklin Watts.
First published in 1998 by Franklin Watts,
96 Leonard Street, London EC2A 4RH, England.
This U. S. edition © 2000 by Gareth Stevens, Inc.
Additional end matter © 2000 by Gareth Stevens, Inc.

Editor: Samantha Armstrong
Series Designer: Kirstie Billingham
Illustrator: Gemini Patel
Religious Education Consultant: Margaret Barratt, M.A., Religious Education lecturer and author
Religious Consultant: Mr. Nazar-e Mustafa, Education Consultant, Central London Mosque
Reading Consultant: Prue Goodwin, Reading and Literacy Centre, Reading

Gareth Stevens Series Editor: Dorothy L. Gibbs

Photographic acknowledgements:
Cover: Steve Shott Photography.
Inside: p. 6 The Hutchison Library; p. 7 H. Rogers, Trip Photographic Library; p. 9 Christine Osborne; p. 11 Trip Photographic Library; p. 23 Abbas/Magnum; p. 27 Abbas/Magnum. All other photographs by Steve Shott Photography.

With thanks to the East London Mosque and the Central London Mosque.

Printed in the United States of America

1 2 3 4 5 6 7 8 9 04 03 02 01 00

# Muslim
## Mosque

Angela Wood

Gareth Stevens Publishing
**MILWAUKEE**

This is one of the symbols used
to represent Islam, the religion of Muslims.

When Muslims use the name of Allah or
the Prophet Muhammad, they show respect by saying,
"Peace and blessings be upon him."

# Contents

Words that appear in the glossary are printed in **boldface**
type the first time they occur in the text.

# Mosques around the World

A **mosque** is a place where Muslims meet to study and to pray to God. There are mosques all around the world.

Muslims also pray at home.

This mosque ▶
is in England.

# Muslim Beliefs

Muslims believe in one God, called **Allah**. Allah sent the angel Gabriel to a man named **Muhammad**, who lived in Arabia. Gabriel told Muhammad that Allah wanted him to be his messenger, or **prophet**. The angel also told him what Allah wanted him to teach others.

There are no pictures or ▶ statues of Allah or the Prophet Muhammad inside a mosque. Instead, the walls and ceilings are decorated with beautiful writing and patterns.

# Prayer Times

Muslims pray five times a day. The exact times they pray change throughout the year. They can go to the mosque at any time, but midday on Fridays is especially important.

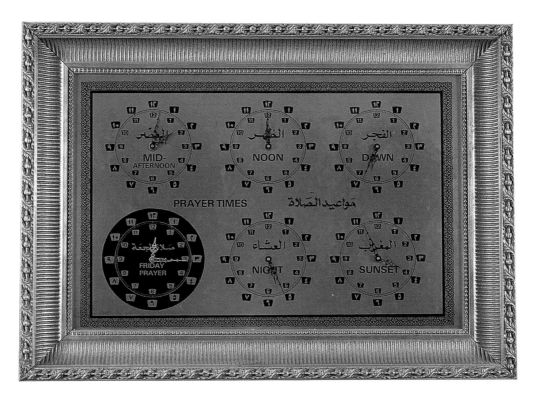

▲ Many mosques have clock boards that show the prayer times for each day. The clocks start at the top of the board on the right-hand side. The dark clock shows the time for midday prayers on a Friday.

8

# The Call to Prayer

When it is time to pray, a man calls out from a **minaret**, which is a tower on or near the mosque. This man is called a **muezzin**. Sometimes his call to prayer is played through a loudspeaker.

This man is a muezzin. ▶
He is calling people to prayer. In some countries, the call to prayer is broadcast on radio and television.

# The Ka'aba

Muslims always face the same direction when they pray. They face toward a building in Saudi Arabia called the **Ka'aba**. The very first offering to Allah was made at the Ka'aba.

The Ka'aba is in the city of **Mecca**. The Prophet Muhammad lived in Mecca and taught people the important messages Allah gave to him.

◀ The Ka'aba, as this model shows, is a cube-shaped building.

Every Muslim tries to ▶ visit Mecca at least once in his or her lifetime. This special visit is called **Hajj**.

10

# Inside a Mosque

The main part of a mosque is the **prayer hall**. In the prayer hall, men and women pray separately. There is no furniture in the hall, but there are carpets or mats for people to kneel or sit on when they pray.

Muslim men are praying ▶ together in a prayer hall. The carpets help them stay in straight lines.

# The Qur'an

Copies of the **Qur'an** are kept inside every mosque. The Qur'an is the special book for Muslims. It is written in **Arabic**. Almost everything Allah told the Prophet Muhammad is written in the Qur'an. This special book is treated with love and **respect**.

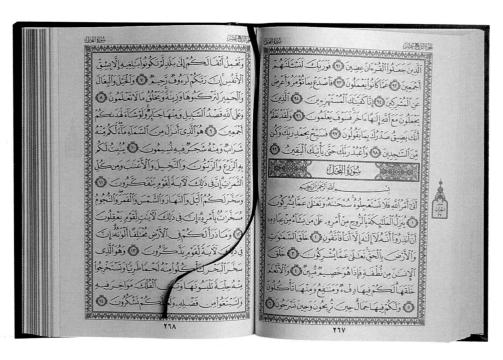

◄ Muslims try to learn the Qur'an by heart.

When the Qur'an is ► read, it is placed on a stand to keep it clean and to show how important it is.

14

# The Mihrab and Minbar

Every mosque has a place called a **mihrab** on one wall. The mihrab shows the direction of the Ka'aba, which is known as **qiblah**. Near the mihrab is a platform called a **minbar**. The **imam**, or prayer leader, stands on the minbar every Friday, at midday, when he speaks to the people.

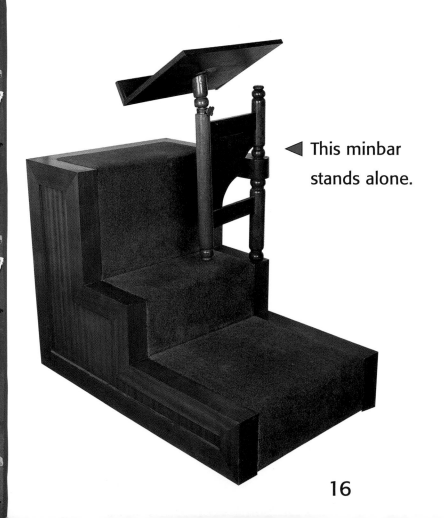

◀ This minbar stands alone.

In this mosque, ▶ the mihrab and the minbar are together. The imam is standing on the minbar facing the people.

# Getting Ready to Pray

When Muslims go into a mosque, they take off their shoes to show their respect. Then they wash themselves carefully.

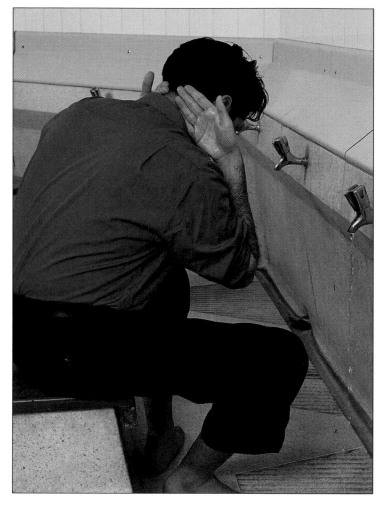

To pray to Allah, being very clean is important. Before Muslims wash, they think of Allah.

The washing is called **wudu**. It is done in a certain order. First, Muslims wash their hands thoroughly.

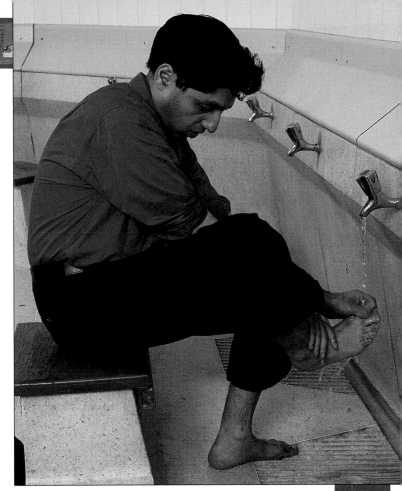

Next, they wash their mouth, nose, face, and arms. Then, they wash their head, neck, and ears. Finally, they wash their feet.

# Prayer Positions

Muslims pray with their whole bodies. They use ten different positions, which, together, are called a **rak'ah**.

◀ Three of the ten Muslim prayer ▶
positions are shown here.
▼

By bending and bowing until their foreheads touch the ground, Muslims show how great Allah is.  At the same time, they say "Allahu Akbar," which means "Allah is the Greatest."

# Muslim Dress

The way Muslims dress is important to show their respect for Allah. Their clothes cover their bodies from the neck to the ankles.

Some Muslim women ▶ and girls keep their heads covered at all times. These Muslim girls all have their heads covered. They are praying together.

22

# Helping Others

Muslims believe they should help other people as much as they can. One way they help others is to give money to charities. Giving money to help others is called **sadaqah**. Doing good deeds is sadaqah, too.

Many mosques have a collection box for gifts of money. Also, once a year, every Muslim family is asked to pay money to help poorer people. This payment is called **zakah**.

This boy is putting ▶ money into the collection box at the mosque.

# A School in a Mosque

Most mosques have classes for children, after school or on weekends. These classes teach the children the Muslim way of life. The children also read the Qur'an and try to learn it by heart.

When they are young, boys and girls study together. When they are older, they have separate classes.

These Muslim girls ▶
are learning the
Arabic language.

# Glossary

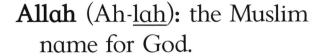

**Allah** (Ah-<u>lah</u>): the Muslim name for God.

**Arabic:** the language spoken in Saudi Arabia and other countries in the Middle East.

**Hajj** (Hadj): the spiritual pilgrimage to Mecca that Muslims have a duty to make at least once in a lifetime.

**imam** (<u>e</u>-mom): the person who leads the prayers in the mosque.

**Ka'aba** (Kah-<u>bah</u>): the cube-shaped building in Mecca toward which Muslims face when they pray.

**Mecca:** the city in Arabia (now Saudi Arabia) where the Prophet Muhammad was born.

**mihrab** (<u>mih</u>-rob): the place on the wall of a prayer hall that shows people the direction to face when they are praying.

**minaret:** the tower on or near a mosque where the muezzin stands to call Muslims to prayer.

**minbar:** a short staircase with a platform on top where the imam stands to talk to the people in a prayer hall.

**mosque** (mahsk): the place Muslims go to pray.

**muezzin** (mo-<u>es</u>-sin): the person who calls Muslims to prayer.

**Muhammad:** the man from Arabia who was called by the angel Gabriel to be the prophet of Allah.

**prayer hall:** the room in a mosque where Muslims pray.

**prophet:** a messenger of God. Muhammad is the Prophet of Allah.

**qiblah** (<u>kih</u>-blah): the direction of the Ka'aba.

**Qur'an** (Coo-<u>rahn</u>): the holy book of Muslims.

**rak'ah** (<u>rahk</u>-ah): a set of ten positions for prayer.

**respect:** thoughtful, considerate, and honorable treatment.

**sadaqah** (<u>sah</u>-dah-kah): good deeds and gifts of money to help others.

**wudu** (woo-doo): washing before prayer.

**zakah** (zah-<u>kah</u>): money paid by Muslim families, once a year, to help poor people.

# More Books to Read

I Am Muslim. *Religions of the World* (series). Jessica Chalfonte (Rosen/Powerkids Press)

Islam. *Discovering Religions* (series). Sue Penney (Raintree Steck-Vaughn)

Mecca. *Holy Cities* (series). Anita Ganeri and Shahrukh Husain (Dillon Press)

Muslim. *Beliefs and Cultures* (series). Richard Tames and Sheila Tames (Children's Press)

Muslim Holidays. Anna O'Mara (Capstone)

Ramadan. Suhaib Hamid Ghazi (Holiday House)

Religion. *Eyewitness Books* (series). Myrtle Langley (Knopf)

The Rise of Islam. John Child (Peter Bedrick Books)

Sacred Myths: Stories of World Religions. Marilyn McFarlane (Sibyl)

Saudi Arabia. *Festivals of the World* (series). Maria O'Shea (Gareth Stevens)

The Story of Religion. Betsy Maestro (Clarion)

What Do We Know About Islam? *What Do We Know About...?* (series). Sharukh Husain (Peter Bedrick Books)

# Videos

*Adam's World Video Set* (12 vols.). (Sound Vision)

*Islam: The Faith and the People.* (United Learning)

*Fatih Sultan Muhammed.* (Islamic Bookstore)

*Taj Mahal: Heaven on Earth.* (United Learning)

# Web Sites

Introduction (teaches Muslim children how to worship) *cairo.spd.louisville.edu/~nevin/Project.html*

The Islamic Garden *home.epix.net/~sarieh/*

Play & Learn Kid's Gallery *playandlearn.org/feature.htm*

Islam for Children *www.jamaat.org/islam/Muhammad.html*

Welcome to Islam *www.jannah.org/slideshow/*

To find additional web sites, use a reliable search engine with one or more of the following keywords: *Allah, imam, Islam, Ka'aba, Koran, Mecca, minaret, mosque, muezzin, Muhammad, Muslim, prophet, Qur'an,* and *religion.*

# Index